BLUE HORSES

BLUE HORSES

MARY OLIVER

THE PENGUIN PRESS

NEW YORK

2014

PENGUIN PRESS
Published by the Penguin Group
Penguin Group (USA) LLC
375 Hudson Street
New York, New York 10014

USA • Canada • UK • Ireland • Australia
New Zealand • India • South Africa • China

penguin.com
A Penguin Random House Company

First published by The Penguin Press,
a member of Penguin Group (USA) LLC, 2014

The following poems were first published in periodicals:
American Scholar: "After Reading Lucretius, I Go to the Pond" (under the
title "Summer Work"); *Appalachia*: "Stebbins Gulch"; *Orion*: "Blueberries":
Parabola: "I'm Not the River," "I'm Feeling Fabulous, Possibly Too Much So.
But I Love It"; *Portland Magazine*: "The Vulture's Wings"

LIBRARY OF CONGRESS CATALOGING-IN-PUBLICATION DATA

Oliver, Mary.
[Poems. Selections]
Blue horses : poems / Mary Oliver.
pages   cm
ISBN 978-1-59420-479-1 (hardback)
I. Title.
PS3565.L5A6   2014b   2014009724
811'.54—dc23

Printed in the United States of America
1   3   5   7   9   10   8   6   4   2

Designed by Amanda Dewey

For Anne Taylor

Contents

If you don't break your ropes while you're alive

do you think

ghosts will do it after?

—KABIR

AFTER READING LUCRETIUS, I GO TO THE POND

The slippery green frog
that went to his death
in the heron's pink throat
was my small brother,

and the heron
with the white plumes
like a crown on his head
who is washing now his great sword-beak
in the shining pond
is my tall thin brother.

My heart dresses in black
and dances.

WHAT I CAN DO

The television has two instruments that control it.
I get confused.
The washer asks me, do you want regular or delicate?
Honestly, I just want clean.
Everything is like that.
I won't even mention cell phones.

I can turn on the light of the lamp beside my chair
where a book is waiting, but that's about it.

Oh yes, and I can strike a match and make fire.

RUMI *(for Coleman Barks)*

When Rumi went into the tavern
I followed.
I heard a lot of crazy talk
and a lot of wise talk.

But the roses wouldn't grow in my hair.

When Rumi left the tavern
I followed.
I don't mean just to peek at
such a famous fellow.
Indeed he was rather ridiculous with his
long beard and his dusty feet.
But I heard less of the crazy talk and
a lot more of the wise talk and I was
hopeful enough to keep listening

until the day I found myself
transformed into an entire garden
of roses.

FIRST YOGA LESSON

"Be a lotus in the pond," she said, "opening
slowly, no single energy tugging
against another but peacefully,
all together."

I couldn't even touch my toes.
"Feel your quadriceps stretching?" she asked.
Well, something was certainly stretching.

Standing impressively upright, she
raised one leg and placed it against
the other, then lifted her arms and
shook her hands like leaves. "Be a tree," she said.

I lay on the floor, exhausted.
But to be a lotus in the pond
opening slowly, and very slowly rising—
that I could do.

I DON'T WANT TO BE DEMURE OR RESPECTABLE

I don't want to be demure or respectable.
I was that way, asleep, for years.
That way, you forget too many important things.
How the little stones, even if you can't hear them,
     are singing.
How the river can't wait to get to the ocean and
     the sky, it's been there before.
What traveling is that!
It is a joy to imagine such distances.
I could skip sleep for the next hundred years.
There is a fire in the lashes of my eyes.
It doesn't matter where I am, it could be a small room.
The glimmer of gold Böhme saw on the kitchen pot
     was missed by everyone else in the house.

Maybe the fire in my lashes is a reflection of that.
Why do I have so many thoughts, they are driving me
     crazy.
Why am I always going anywhere, instead of
     somewhere?
Listen to me or not, it hardly matters.
I'm not trying to be wise, that would be foolish.
I'm just chattering.

STEBBIN'S GULCH

by the randomness
of the way
the rocks tumbled
ages ago

the water pours
it pours
it pours
ever along the slant

of downgrade
dashing its silver thumbs
against the rocks
or pausing to carve

a sudden curled space
where the flashing fish
splash or drowse
while the kingfisher overhead

rattles and stares
and so it continues for miles

this bolt of light,
its only industry

to descend
and to be beautiful
while it does so;
as for purpose

there is none,
it is simply
one of those gorgeous things
that was made

to do what it does perfectly
and to last,
as almost nothing does,
almost forever.

NO MATTER WHAT

No matter what the world claims,
its wisdom always growing, so it's said,
some things don't alter with time:
the first kiss is a good example,
and the flighty sweetness of rhyme.

No matter what the world preaches
spring unfolds in its appointed time,
the violets open and the roses,
snow in its hour builds its shining curves,
there's the laughter of children at play,
and the wholesome sweetness of rhyme.

No matter what the world does,
some things don't alter with time.
The first kiss, the first death.
The sorrowful sweetness of rhyme.

ANGELS

You might see an angel anytime
and anywhere. Of course you have
to open your eyes to a kind of
second level, but it's not really
hard. The whole business of
what's reality and what isn't has
never been solved and probably
never will be. So I don't care to
be too definite about anything.
I have a lot of edges called Perhaps
and almost nothing you can call
Certainty. For myself, but not
for other people. That's a place
you just can't get into, not
entirely anyway, other people's
heads.

I'll just leave you with this.
I don't care how many angels can
dance on the head of a pin. It's
enough to know that for some people
they exist, and that they dance.

WHAT WE WANT

In a poem
people want
something fancy,

but even more
they want something
inexplicable
made plain,

easy to swallow—
not unlike a suddenly
harmonic passage

in an otherwise
difficult and sometimes dissonant
symphony—

even if it is only
for the moment
of hearing it.

IF I WANTED A BOAT

I would want a boat, if I wanted a
boat, that bounded hard on the waves,
that didn't know starboard from port
and wouldn't learn, that welcomed
dolphins and headed straight for the
whales, that, when rocks were close,
would slide in for a touch or two,
that wouldn't keep land in sight and
went fast, that leaped into the spray.
What kind of life is it always to plan
and do, to promise and finish, to wish
for the near and the safe? Yes, by the
heavens, if I wanted a boat I would want
a boat I couldn't steer.

GOOD MORNING

1.

"Hello, wren" is the first thing I say.
"Where did you come from appearing so
sudden and cheerful in the privet? Which,
by the way, has decided to decorate itself
in so many white blossoms."

2.

Paulus is coming to visit! Paulus the
dancer, the potter. Who is just beginning
his eightieth decade, who walks without
shoes in the woods because his feet, he
says, ask to be in touch with the earth.
Paulus who when he says my poems sometimes
changes them a little, according to the
occasion or his own feelings. Okay, I say.

3.

Stay young, always, in the theater of your
mind.

4.

Bless the notebook that I always carry in
    my pocket.
And the pen.
Bless the words with which I try to say
    what I see, think, or feel.
With gratitude for the grace of the earth.
The expected and the exception, both.
For all the hours I have been given to
    be in this world.

5.

The multiplicity of forms! The hummingbird,
the fox, the raven, the sparrow hawk, the
otter, the dragonfly, the water lily! And
on and on. It must be a great disappointment
to God if we are not dazzled at least ten
times a day.

6.

Slowly the morning climbs toward the day.
As for the poem, not this poem but any
poem, do you feel its sting? Do you feel
its hope, its entrance to a community? Do
you feel its hand in your hand?

7.

But perhaps you're still sleeping. I
could wake you with a touch or a kiss.
But so could I shake the petals from
the wild rose which blossoms so silently
and perfectly, and I do not.

THE WASP

Why the wasp was on my bed I didn't
know. Why I was in bed I did know. Why
there wasn't room for both of us I
didn't know. I watched it idly. Idleness
can be a form of dying, I did know that.

The wasp didn't communicate how it felt.
It did look confused on the white sheet,
as though it had landed somewhere in the
Arctic. And it did flick its wings when
I raised my legs, causing an upheaval.

I didn't want to be lying there. I didn't
want to be going in that direction. And
so I say it was a gift when it rose into
the air and, as wasps do, expressed itself
in a sudden and well-aimed motion.

Almost delicious was its deep, inflexible
sting.

BLUEBERRIES

I'm living in a warm place now, where
you can purchase fresh blueberries all
year long. Labor free. From various
countries in South America. They're
as sweet as any, and compared with the
berries I used to pick in the fields
outside of Provincetown, they're
enormous. But berries are berries. They
don't speak any language I can't
understand. Neither do I find ticks or
small spiders crawling among them. So,
generally speaking, I'm very satisfied.

There are limits, however. What they
don't have is the field. The field they
belonged to and through the years I
began to feel I belonged to. Well,
there's life, and then there's later.
Maybe it's myself that I miss. The
field, and the sparrow singing at the
edge of the woods. And the doe that one
morning came upon me unaware, all

tense and gorgeous. She stamped her hoof
as you would to any intruder. Then gave
me a long look, as if to say, Okay, you
stay in your patch, I'll stay in mine.
Which is what we did. Try packing that
up, South America.

LITTLE LORD LOVE

Little Lord Love, he with the arrows,
has definitely shot the last one
    with my name on it
straight to the heart
now, when I'm no longer young
and it's not so easy to stay up half the night
talking, and so on.

Little Lord, frolicsome boy,
why did you wait until now?

LITTLE CRAZY LOVE SONG

I don't want eventual,
I want soon.
It's 5 a.m. It's noon.
It's dusk falling to dark.
I listen to music.
I eat up a few wild poems
while time creeps along
as though it's got all day.
This is what I have.
The dull hangover of waiting,
the blush of my heart on the damp grass,
the flower-faced moon.
A gull broods on the shore
where a moment ago there were two.
Softly my right hand fondles my left hand
as though it were you.

I WOKE

I woke
and crept
like a cat

on silent feet
about my own house—
to look

at you
while you were sleeping,
your hair

sprayed on the pillow,
your eyes
closed,

your body
safe and solitary,
and my doors

shut for your safety
and your comfort.
I did this

thinking I was intruding,
yet wanting to see
the most beautiful thing

that has ever been in my house.

THE MANGROVES

As I said before, I am living now
in a warm place, surrounded by
mangroves. Mostly I walk beside
them, they discourage entrance.
The black oaks and the pines
of my northern home are in my heart,
even as I hear them whisper, "Listen,
we are trees too." Okay, I'm trying. They
certainly put on an endless performance
of leaves. Admiring is easy, but affinity,
that does take some time. So many
and so leggy and all of them rising as if
attempting to escape this world which, don't
they know it, can't be done. "Are you
trying to fly or what?" I ask, and they
answer back, "We are what we are, you
are what you are, love us if you can."

THE HUMMINGBIRDS

In this book
    there are many hummingbirds—
the blue-throated, the bumblebee, the calliope,
    the cinnamon, the lucifer, and of course
        the ruby-throated.
Imagine!
Well, that's all you can do.
For they're swift as the wind

and they fly, not across the pages but,
like many shy and otherworldly things,
    between them.
I know you'll keep looking now that I've told you.
I'm hungry to see them too, but I can't
    hold them back even for a moment, they're
        busy, as all things are, with their own lives.
So all I can do is let you know
    they're here somewhere.
All I can do is tell you
    by putting my own hunger on the page.

SUCH SILENCE

As deep as I ever went into the forest
I came upon an old stone bench, very, very old,
and around it a clearing, and beyond that
trees taller and older than I had ever seen.

Such silence!
It really wasn't so far from a town, but it seemed
all the clocks in the world had stopped counting.
So it was hard to suppose the usual rules applied.

Sometimes there's only a hint, a possibility.
What's magical, sometimes, has deeper roots
    than reason.
I hope everyone knows that.

I sat on the bench, waiting for something.
An angel, perhaps.
Or dancers with the legs of goats.

No, I didn't see either. But only, I think, because
    I didn't stay long enough.

WATERING THE STONES

Every summer I gather a few stones from
the beach and keep them in a glass bowl.
Now and again I cover them with water,
and they drink. There's no question about
this; I put tinfoil over the bowl, tightly,
yet the water disappears. This doesn't
mean we ever have a conversation, or that
they have the kind of feelings we do, yet
it might mean something. Whatever the
stones are, they don't lie in the water
and do nothing.

Some of my friends refuse to believe it
happens, even though they've seen it. But
a few others—I've seen them walking down
the beach holding a few stones, and they
look at them rather more closely now.
Once in a while, I swear, I've even heard
one or two of them saying "Hello."
Which, I think, does no harm to anyone or
anything, does it?

FRANZ MARC'S BLUE HORSES

I step into the painting of the four blue horses.
I am not even surprised that I can do this.

One of the horses walks toward me.
His blue nose noses me lightly. I put my arm
over his blue mane, not holding on, just
    commingling.
He allows me my pleasure.
Franz Marc died a young man, shrapnel in his brain.
I would rather die than try to explain to the blue horses
    what war is.
They would either faint in horror, or simply
    find it impossible to believe.
I do not know how to thank you, Franz Marc.
Maybe our world will grow kinder eventually.
Maybe the desire to make something beautiful
    is the piece of God that is inside each of us.
Now all four horses have come closer,
    are bending their faces toward me
        as if they have secrets to tell.
I don't expect them to speak, and they don't.
If being so beautiful isn't enough, what
    could they possibly say?

THE VULTURE'S WINGS

The vulture's
wings are
black death
color but
the underwings
as sunlight
flushes into
the feathers
are bright
are swamped
with light.
Just something
explainable by
the sun's
angle yet
I keep
looking I
keep wondering
standing so
far below
these high
floating birds

could this
as most
things do
be offering
something for
us to
think about
seriously?

ON MEDITATING, SORT OF

Meditation, so I've heard, is best accomplished
if you entertain a certain strict posture.
Frankly, I prefer just to lounge under a tree.
So why should I think I could ever be successful?

Some days I fall asleep, or land in that
even better place—half-asleep—where the world,
spring, summer, autumn, winter—
flies through my mind in its
hardy ascent and its uncompromising descent.

So I just lie like that, while distance and time
reveal their true attitudes: they never
heard of me, and never will, or ever need to.

Of course I wake up finally
thinking, how wonderful to be who I am,
made out of earth and water,
my own thoughts, my own fingerprints—
all that glorious, temporary stuff.

TO BE HUMAN IS TO SING YOUR OWN SONG

Everything I can think of that my parents
thought or did I don't think and I don't do.
I opened windows, they shut them. I pulled
open the curtains, they shut them. If you
get my drift. Of course there were some
similarities—they wanted to be happy and
they weren't. I wanted to be Shelley and I
wasn't. I don't mean I didn't have to avoid
imitation, the gloom was pretty heavy. But
then, for me, there was the forest, where
they didn't exist. And the fields. Where I
learned about birds and other sweet tidbits
of existence. The song sparrow, for example.

In the song sparrow's nest the nestlings,
those who would sing eventually, must listen
carefully to the father bird as he sings
and make their own song in imitation of his.
I don't know if any other bird does this (in
nature's way has to do this). But I know a
child doesn't have to. Doesn't have to.
Doesn't have to. And I didn't.

LONELINESS

I too have known loneliness.
I too have known what it is to feel
    misunderstood,
    rejected, and suddenly
not at all beautiful.
Oh, mother earth,
    your comfort is great, your arms never withhold.
It has saved my life to know this.
Your rivers flowing, your roses opening in the morning.
Oh, motions of tenderness!

DRIFTING

I was enjoying everything: the rain, the path
    wherever it was taking me, the earth roots
    beginning to stir.
I didn't intend to start thinking about God,
    it just happened.
How God, or the gods, are invisible,
    quite understandable.
But holiness is visible, entirely.
It's wonderful to walk along like that,
    thought not the usual intention to reach an answer
    but merely drifting.
Like clouds that only seem weightless
    but of course are not.
Are really important.
I mean, terribly important.
Not decoration by any means.
By next week the violets will be blooming.
Anyway, this was my delicious walk in the rain.
What was it actually about?

Think about what it is that music is trying to say.
It was something like that.

FORGIVE ME

Angels are wonderful but they are so, well, aloof.
It's what I sense in the mud and the roots of the
trees, or the well, or the barn, or the rock with
its citron map of lichen that halts my feet and
makes my eyes flare, feeling the presence of some
spirit, some small god, who abides there.

If I were a perfect person, I would be bowing
continuously.
I'm not, though I pause wherever I feel this
holiness, which is why I'm often so late coming
back from wherever I went.

Forgive me.

I'M FEELING FABULOUS, POSSIBLY TOO MUCH SO.
BUT I LOVE IT

It's spring and Mockingbird is teaching himself
    new ways to celebrate.
If you can imagine that—that gusty talker.
And the sky is painting itself a brand-new
    robust blue
plenty of which is spilling into the pond.
I don't weigh very much, but right now
I weigh nothing.
And my mind is, I guess you would say, compounded.
One voice is saying, Ah, it's Mockingbird.
Another voice is saying, The pond never looked
    this blue before.
Another voice says, There couldn't be a more
    splendid world, and here I am
        existing in it.
I think, just for the joy of it, I'll fly.
I believe I could.

And yet another voice says, Can we come down
    from the clouds now?
And some other voice answers, Okay.
    But only for a while.

ON NOT MOWING THE LAWN

Let the grass spring up tall, let its roots sing
  and the seeds begin their scattering.
Let the weeds rejoin and be prolific throughout.
Let the noise of the mower be banished, hurrah!
Let the path become where I choose to walk, and not
  otherwise established.
Let the goldfinches be furnished their humble dinner.
Let the sparrows determine their homes in security.
Let the honeysuckle reach as high as my window, that it
  may look in.
Let the mice fill their barns and bins with a sufficiency.
Let anything created, that wants to creep or leap
  forward,
    be able to do so.
Let the grasshopper have gliding space.
Let the noise of the mower be banished, yes, yes.
Let the katydid return and announce himself in the
  long evenings.
Let the blades of grass surge back from the last
  cutting.
Or, if you want to be poetic: the leaves of grass.

THE FOURTH SIGN OF THE ZODIAC

1.

Why should I have been surprised?
Hunters walk the forest
without a sound.
The hunter, strapped to his rifle,
the fox on his feet of silk,
the serpent on his empire of muscles—
all move in a stillness,
hungry, careful, intent.
Just as the cancer
entered the forest of my body,
without a sound.

2.

The question is,
what will it be like
after the last day?
Will I float
into the sky
or will I fray
within the earth or a river—
remembering nothing?
How desperate I would be
if I couldn't remember
the sun rising, if I couldn't
remember trees, rivers; if I couldn't
even remember, beloved,
your beloved name.

3.

I know, you never intended to be in this world.
But you're in it all the same.

So why not get started immediately.

I mean, belonging to it.
There is so much to admire, to weep over.

And to write music or poems about.

Bless the feet that take you to and fro.
Bless the eyes and the listening ears.
Bless the tongue, the marvel of taste.
Bless touching.

You could live a hundred years, it's happened.
Or not.
I am speaking from the fortunate platform
of many years,
none of which, I think, I ever wasted.
Do you need a prod?
Do you need a little darkness to get you going?
Let me be as urgent as a knife, then,
and remind you of Keats,
so single of purpose and thinking, for a while,
he had a lifetime.

4.

Late yesterday afternoon, in the heat,
all the fragile blue flowers in bloom
in the shrubs in the yard next door had
tumbled from the shrubs and lay
wrinkled and fading in the grass. But
this morning the shrubs were full of
the blue flowers again. There wasn't
a single one on the grass. How, I
wondered, did they roll or crawl back
to the shrubs and then back up to
the branches, that fiercely wanting,
as we all do, just a little more of
life?

TO SHIVA

Shiva, pretend you are with me
as the doe in her summer-red coat
tiptoes
    down
        through the pines
            and enters the pasture.

She neither hurries nor hesitates.
She knows exactly how carefully it must be done.

Shiva, I know the odds.

If the fawn is where she left it, the world
    in that moment goes on being created.
And if the fawn has vanished, it is the destroyer's hour.

Lord of Life and of Death,
I just wanted you to stand here for a moment
    not like a god but like a mortal being
to see for yourself how the doe
    carefully
        vanishes
            into the grass

and when she emerges how the heart leaps joyful
if the world steps out beside her. That little dancer
    still licking milk from its lip.

OWL POEM

One has to say this for the rounds of life
    that keep coming and going; it has worked so far.
The rabbit, after all, has never asked if the grass
    wanted to live.
Any more than the owl consults with the rabbit.

Acceptance of the world requires
    that I bow even to you,
Master of the night.

A LITTLE ADO ABOUT THIS AND THAT

If I walk out into the world in irritation or
self-centerness, the birds scatter.

I would like people to remember of me, how
inexhaustible was her mindfulness.

The hurricane may find us or it will not, that
will always be the way.

With Shelley, I feel the visceral experience
of imagination.

Can you imagine anyone having a "casual" faith?

"This is what I know from years of being me," said
a friend.

You will always love me.

About God, how could he give up his secrets and
still be God?

If you think you see a face in the clouds, why not
send a greeting? It can't do any harm.

DO STONES FEEL?

Do stones feel?
Do they love their life?
Or does their patience drown out everything else?

When I walk on the beach I gather a few
        white ones, dark ones, the multiple colors.
Don't worry, I say, I'll bring you back, and I do.

Is the tree as it rises delighted with its many
        branches,
each one like a poem?

Are the clouds glad to unburden their bundles of rain?

Most of the world says no, no, it's not possible.

I refuse to think to such a conclusion.
Too terrible it would be, to be wrong.

I'M NOT THE RIVER

I'm not the river
that powerful presence.
And I'm not the black oak tree
which is patience personified.
And I'm not redbird
who is a brief life heartily enjoyed.
Nor am I mud nor rock nor sand
which is holding everything together.
No, I am none of these meaningful things, not yet.

THE OAK TREE LOVES PATIENCE

The oak tree
    loves patience,
the mountain is
    still looking,

as it has for centuries,
    for a word to say about
the gradual way it
    slides itself

back to the
    world below
to begin again,
    in another life,

to be fertile.
    When the wind blows
the grass
    whistles and whispers

in myths and riddles
    and not in our language

but one far older.
    The sea is the sea is

always the sea.
    These things
you can count on
    as you walk about the world

happy or sad,
    talky or silent, making
weapons, love, poems.
    The briefest of fires.

THE COUNTRY OF THE TREES

There is no king in their country
and there is no queen
and there are no princes vying for power,
　　inventing corruption.
Just as with us many children are born
and some will live and some will die and the country
　　will continue.

The weather will always be important.

And there will always be room for the weak, the violets
　　and the bloodroot.
When it is cold they will be given blankets of leaves.
When it is hot they will be given shade.
And not out of guilt, neither for a year-end deduction
　　but maybe for the cheer of their colors, their
　　　　small flower faces.

They are not like us.

Some will perish to become houses or barns,
　　fences and bridges.

Others will endure past the counting of years.
And none will ever speak a single word of complaint,
    as though language, after all,
did not work well enough, was only an early stage.
Neither do they ever have any questions to the gods—
    which one is the real one, and what is the plan.
As though they have been told everything already,
    and are content.

WHAT GORGEOUS THING

I do not know what gorgeous thing
        the bluebird keeps saying,
his voice easing out of his throat,
        beak, body into the pink air
of the early morning. I like it
        whatever it is. Sometimes
it seems the only thing in the world
        that is without dark thoughts.
Sometimes it seems the only thing
        in the world that is without
questions that can't and probably
        never will be answered, the
only thing that is entirely content
        with the pink, then clear white
morning and, gratefully, says so.

Note

Franz Marc was born in Munich in 1880. He was a part of the Blue Rider group of painters, to which Wassily Kandinsky also belonged. In 1916, while serving in the army, he was struck in the temple by shrapnel and fatally wounded. He was 36 years old.

Acknowledgments

My thanks to the editors of the following magazines in which some of the poems previously appeared.

American Scholar, "After Reading Lucretius, I go to the
     Pond" (under the title "Summer Work.")
Portland Magazine, "The Vulture's Wings"
Appalachia, "Stebbins Gulch"
Parabola, "I'm Not the River" and "I'm Feeling
     Fabulous, Possibly Too Much So. But I Love It"
Orion, "Blueberries"

Some of the lines in "The Fourth Sign of the Zodiac" (poem 3) I "borrowed" from a poem previously published in *Five Points.*